Fun Facts about the Summer and Winter Olympic Games

SPORTS BOOK GRADE 3

Children's Sports & Outdoors Books

BABY PROFESSOR
EDUCATION KIDS

Speedy Publishing LLC

40 E. Main St. #1156

Newark, DE 19711

www.speedypublishing.com

Copyright 2017

For athletes, one of the greatest honors is to represent their countries in the Olympic Games. Let's learn some record-breaking facts about the Olympics!

OLYMPIC FLAG

WHAT ARE THE OLYMPICS?

The history of the Olympic Games goes back into classical Greek history. The original Olympics were a religious festival. People from different Greek city-states honored the gods by competing in events like running, wrestling, and throwing the discus or the javelin.

➲ The original series of Olympic Games took place every four years in Olympia, Greece for about one thousand years, from 776 BCE to 393 CE.

- If Greek cities were fighting each other at the time of the Olympics, as often happened, there was a special truce so the best athletes could take part in the games.

- The first event was a race of women to see who would be the "queen" of the games! All the other events were for men only.

ANCIENT GREEK OLYMPICS

LAUREL WREATH IN THREE DIFFERENT COLORS - GOLD, SILVER AND BRONZE, AWARDED TO THE TOP THREE COMPETITORS

➲ The winners in the original games were honored and got to wear a crown made of olive leaves, but there was no Olympic medal or other trophy.

JAVELIN THROWERS OF ANCIENT GREECE

➲ For most of the original Olympics, the athletes competed naked!

1896 OLYMPIC OPENING CEREMONY

In the nineteenth century there was a movement to revise the Olympic Games as a peaceful competition between nations. A French teacher, Baron Pierre de Coubertin, proposed the revival at a meeting in Paris in 1894.

➲ The first Olympics in the new series were in 1896 in Athens, Greece. Fourteen nations took part, and athletes from ten nations won medals. Greece, the host country, won 47 medals, more than any other country.

⊃ Baron de Coubertin designed the Olympic flag in 1914. Its five rings represent five major regions of the world: The Americas, Africa, Asia, Europe, and Oceana (including countries like Australia and New Zealand).

BARON DE COUBERTIN

LAWTON REDMAN 2002 WINTER OLYMPICS

➡ The Olympics only included summer sports until 1924, when the Winter Olympics began. The Winter Olympics were based on an earlier competition called The Nordic Games.

ELI BREMER IN 2008 SUMMER OLYMPICS MODERN PENTATHLON SHOW JUMPING EVENT

⊃ Until 1994 the summer and winter Olympics took place in the same year. From then on, the summer and winter games have alternated every two years.

- Only four athletes have won medals at both the summer and winter Olympics.

- Until 1912 the gold medals for winners were, well, gold! Since then, they have been silver with a gold covering.

OLYMPIC GOLD MEDALS

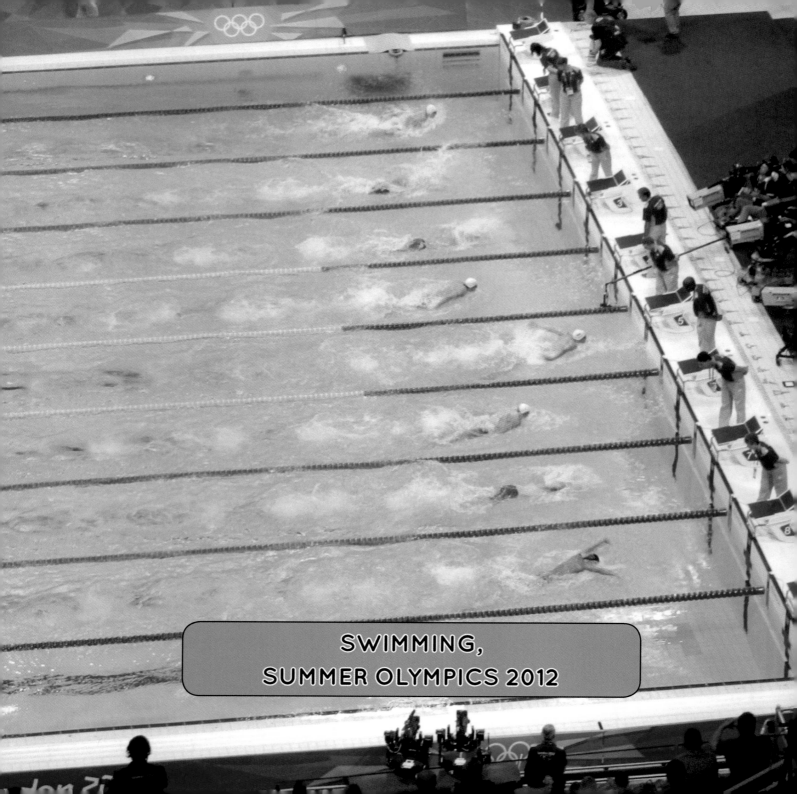

SWIMMING,
SUMMER OLYMPICS 2012

THE SUMMER OLYMPICS

Summer Olympic sports include track and field events like running and jumping competitions, swimming events, team sports like soccer and field hockey, and individual sports ranging from archery to weightlifting.

Here are some fun facts about the summer Olympics.

- **Michael Phelps** of the United States has won 28 Olympic medals, the most for a man. Larrisa Latynina, from the former Soviet Union, won 18 medals, tops for a woman.

REFUGEE OLYMPIC TEAM

- In the 2016 Olympics in Brazil, a team of ten refugees from several nations competed as the "Refugee Olympic Team".

TEAM USA DURING 2008 SUMMER OLYMPICS

- The United States has won more Summer Olympic medals than any other country, with over two thousand.

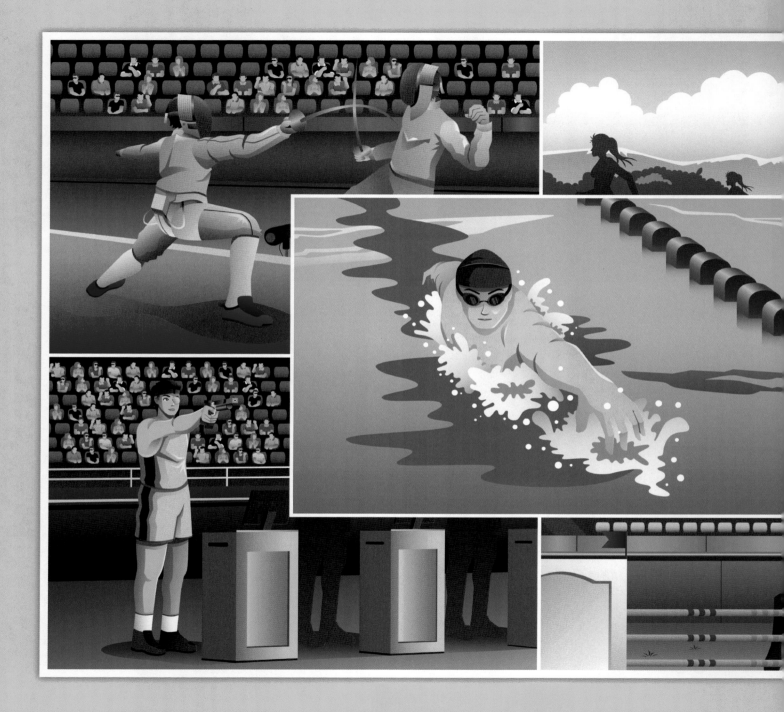

○ Perhaps the toughest event is the pentathlon. Each competitor has to be excellent at shooting, fencing, swimming, show jumping (on a horse), and running. The event is supposed to show off the skills of a messenger who has to carry important news over rough terrain and past the enemies who try to stop him.

In the 1900 Olympics in Paris a boy helped the Dutch rowing team in a race, serving as their coxswain at the last moment. He was about ten years old—but nobody thought to get his name, so we don't know who he was!

ROWING AT THE 2004 SUMMER OLYMPICS

BIKILA AT THE REAR OF THE SIX-MAN LEAD
PACK NEAR THE 10-KILOMETRE

- In 1960, Abebe Bikila of Ethiopia was the first African to win the Olympic marathon race—and he ran barefoot!

- On the other hand, a marathon runner in the 1904 Olympics in Saint Louis was disqualified for cheating. It turned out he had gotten a ride in a car for most of the distance of the race, and only ran the last four miles.

- Early Olympics had competition for arts events, as well as sports. Baron de Coubertin, who helped start the modern Olympics, won the gold medal for literature in 1912.

MARTIN KLEIN (PAREMAL) JA ALFRED ASIKAINEN (1912)

- At the 1912 Olympics, there was a wrestling match that lasted more than eleven hours. Martin Klein of Russia finally defeated Alfred Asikainen of Finland, but then he was too tired to go on and compete in the finals!

- James Connolly was a student at Harvard College in Massachusetts in 1895. He asked permission to take a leave of absence from his studies so he could compete in the first modern Olympics, and the college said no. So Connolly dropped out of school, went to Athens, and won first place in his event. Harvard later offered him an honorary degree, and he turned it down.

JAMES CONNOLLY

NADIA COMANECI MONTREAL 1976

- Nadia Comaneci was an excellent Romanian gymnast. She was so good that she got a perfect score of 10.0 from all the judges in one competition. They had not designed the scoreboard to show a score that high, since nobody had thought such perfection was possible, so they had to show her score as "1" instead of "10"!

WINTER OLYMPICS FOR WINTER SPORTS

Winter Olympics events include team events like hockey and curling, racing sports like speed skating and various skiing events, and style events like figure skating. Here are some cool Winter Olympics facts:

- Ole Einar Bjørndalen of Norway has won more Winter Olympics medals than anyone else, with 13.

- Over 1300 medals get awarded during the course of each Winter Olympics.

OLE EINAR BJØRNDALEN
KONTIOLAHTI 2012

ANDERS HAUGEN

- Anders Haugen competed in the 1924 Olympics in ski-jumping. There was an error in the scoring which was not discovered until 50 years later. When the error was corrected, Haugen, 83 years old by then, suddenly became a medal winner and got to receive his medal!

- Artificial snow was used for the first time at the Winter Olympics in Lake Placid, New York in 1980. With global warming advancing, the need to maintain ice surfaces and snow slopes by artificial means is increasing!

NORWEGIAN MEN'S 4 X 10 KILOMETRE RELAY TEAM AT 2010 WINTER GAMES

- Athletes from Norway have won more medals than Winter Olympics athletes from any other country.

The youngest winner of Winter Olympics gold was Tara Lipinski, who was 15 at the 1998 Winter Olympics in Japan.

THE PARALYMPICS

In 1948 a doctor in Great Britain started an event for British war veterans who had suffered spinal injuries during World War II, between 1939 and 1945. The event grew and expanded to become a major international sports event. The Paralympics now takes place in coordination with the Summer and Winter Olympics, although with a much smaller budget.

Paralympic athletes have a wide range of disabilities that might impair their muscle power, their range of movement, or their vision. Some are missing limbs or have other physical or intellectual challenges.

Despite these challenges, competitors take part in sports of all sorts. The rules of some sports, like basketball, have been adjusted for teams in wheelchairs or using other aids. Blind runners often compete with a sighted companion to make sure they can stay on the course.

- In 1948, the first event in what became the Paralympics was an archery competition for veterans of World War II who had suffered spinal cord injuries. Sixteen British veterans took part.

- In 1952 Dutch athletes joined in.

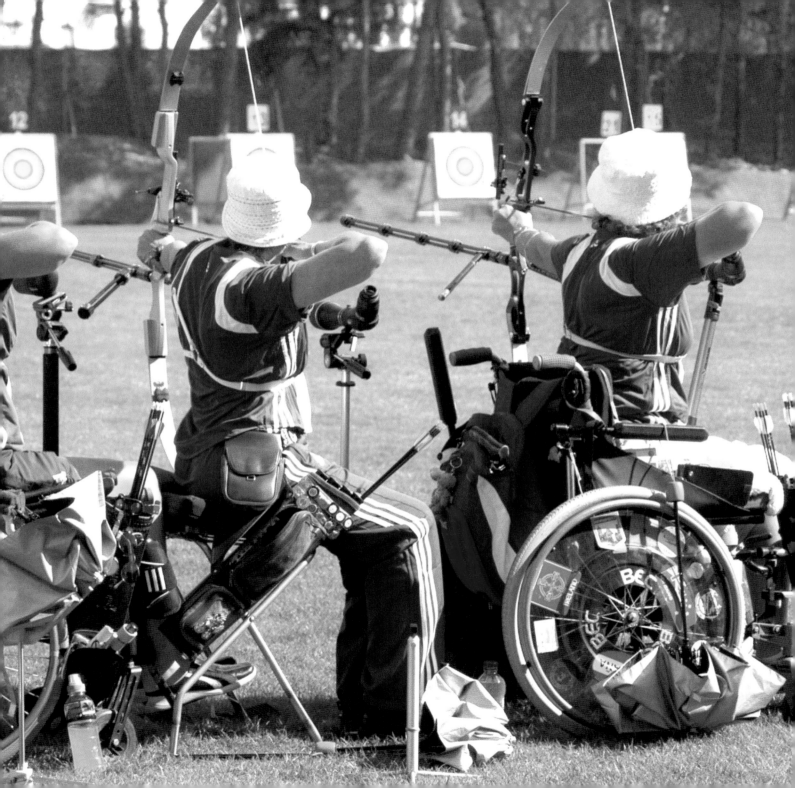

- The games' name originally referred to the fact that most competitors were dealing with some sort of paralysis. Athletes with other disabilities now compete, starting with the 1976 games in Toronto, Canada. Now the name is said to show that these games are "in parallel" with the Summer and Winter Olympics.

- Athletes with disabilities sometimes competed in the regular Olympics before the Paralympics became available. United States gymnast George Eyser, competing in the 1904 Olympics with an artificial leg, won three gold medals—all on the same day!

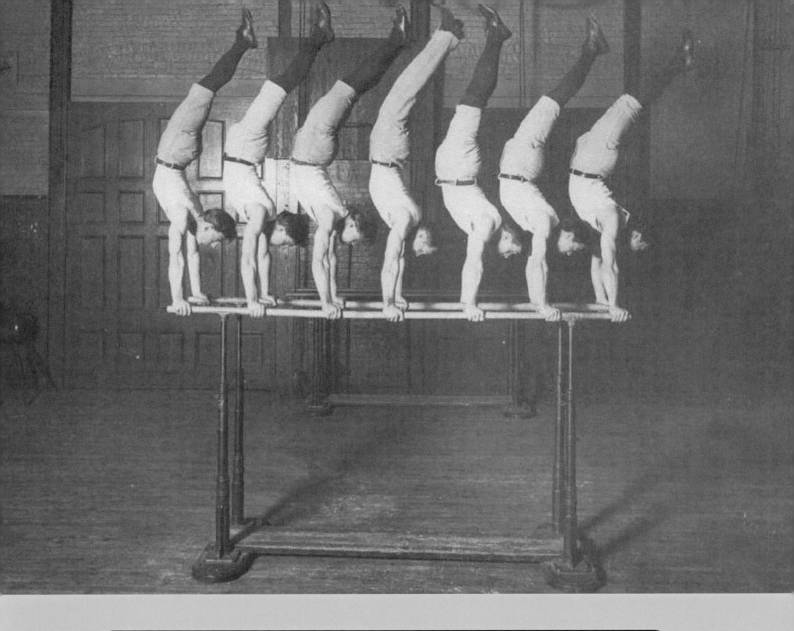

CONCORDIA TURNVEREIN GYMNASTIC TEAM, 1908, GEORGE EYSER

TANNI-GREY THOMPSON

○ Tanni-Grey Thompson of Great Britain competed in the Paralympics between 1988 and 2004. She won 16 medals, eleven of them gold, in wheelchair races of various lengths, and in basketball.

○ Trischa Zorn, a swimmer from the United States, is the top medal-winner in the Paralympics. She has won 55 medals, of which 41 are gold!

THE FUTURE OF THE OLYMPICS

In the coming years the Winter Olympics will be held in 2018 in PyeonChang, South Korea, and in 2022 in Beinjing, China. The next Summer Olympics will be in 2020 in Tokyo, Japan.

The long-term future of the Olympics is a little uncertain. The event is so expensive to put on that fewer and fewer cities want to bid for the right to host it.

PYEONGCHANG WINS BID TO HOST 2018
WINTER OLYMPICS

There is a movement to make Greece once again the permanent home of at least the Summer Olympics, so that the stadiums, swimming and racing facilities, and even housing for the athletes could be reused over many years, rather than city after city having to build an expensive complex of facilities for a single event.

THE WORLD OF SPORTS

Run, jump, and play! Doing sports is not only fun, it helps you develop a healthy, agile body and even helps keep your mind alert. And, who knows? You might make it to the Olympics yourself one day!

Read more about the world of sports in Baby Professor books like *Amazing Facts about the Science of Sports*, *Women who Dominated in Sports*, and *The Legends of Sports: Tiger Woods, Michael Jordan and Muhammad Ali*.

Visit

BABY PROFESSOR
EDUCATION KIDS

www.BabyProfessorBooks.com

to download Free Baby Professor eBooks
and view our catalog of new and exciting
Children's Books

Made in the USA
Columbia, SC
31 March 2020